T0063159

Hey Waitress, Over Here!

Helen Marie Bentz

Order this book online at www.trafford.com
or email orders@trafford.com

Most Trafford titles are also available at major online book retailers.

Printed in the United States of America.

ISBN: 978-1-4120-7028-7 (sc)
ISBN: 978-1-4669-7659-7 (e)

Library of Congress Control Number: 2012922619

Trafford rev. 02/22/2013

 www.trafford.com

North America & international
toll-free: 1 888 232 4444 (USA & Canada)
phone: 250 383 6864 ♦ fax: 812 355 4082

Contents

Dedication

I wish to dedicate this book to two employers I have had in the past, Sandy Margist and Bill Gamuciello and my present employer, John Stant.

I also want to thank Mike Kulhanek who has a lot of faith in me.

Many thanks to my daughter-in-law, Naomi Bentz, who helped me with the book and a big thank you to my brother, Roger Goldsborough who did a lot to get this book together for me, and also thank you to Lorie Hallberg for all of her help.

Introduction

Have you ever wondered what an exciting life restaurant work is? In reality, no two days are ever exactly the same.

Some things are hilarious, other things are interesting and still other things bring a smile to a person's face.

What about sad things that make a person want to cry?

I have even seen dirty restaurants and I also know about robberies!

Yes, I have seen many things since I started working in restaurants in the mid 1960's, but oh, how I wish I had kept a record of all those things!

This book is about things I have personally witnessed or things other people have told me about, but everything is true.

I hope you will enjoy reading this book as much as I have enjoyed writing it, so kick your shoes off and sit back and be ready for all the exciting things in this book.

Chapter One

Funny And Amusing Things

This chapter is entitled Funny & Amusing Things because quite simply, if it doesn't tickle your funny bone, it will certainly bring a smile to your face.

No person's name or restaurant name is given to protect those guilty of making us laugh.

I STARTED DOING waitress work in the 1960's when I was sixteen. I worked in the local restaurant and it seemed to me that it was the place where everyone worked at some time or another.

My employer frowned upon credit cards so, for his wife to own a credit card was a "no-no." One day she applied for a credit card & got it without her husband's knowledge and she felt so important. She didn't intend to ever use the credit card, but she really enjoyed having it.

When I was a teenager, my best friend and I passed silly notes in study hall and really the notes probably would not have made much sense to anyone who would have read them.

My employer's wife had heart surgery and she was in the hospital for a while. Even though heart surgery is serious even today, it was even more serious in the 1960's. My how the medical field has advanced today!

When my employer's wife was in the hospital, I wrote her a silly letter that was actually twenty one pages long! Yes, that's right twenty one pages long! I had written silly things like, "Don't go away. I'll be right back! Well I'm back now. I just had to get a drink of water!"

Imagine my surprise when many years later she told me she still had that letter. She said when she received my letter in the hospital and as she was reading my letter, she laughed until she cried. The laughter did her so much good that she told me she was sure it helped speed her recovery.

As she was telling me this many years later, she was still laughing and had tears rolling down her cheeks. It really made my day to see her laugh that hard about my letter all those years later.

What surprised me even more was that a year after she had died, her husband told me he still had that letter and he was telling me how much his wife had really enjoyed it too.

Apparently, he had enjoyed my letter too, because he was laughing as he was talking to me.

One day a customer blew his nose and he blew his nose so loudly that I heard it echo in the restaurant.

In one restaurant I had worked, the owner was told that the server's were nowhere in sight when customers came in. This was a bad thing anytime, to not see any employee, because this left the cash register unattended, but this was between midnight and eight in the morning. The owner of the restaurant was told this more than once. It was discovered that the employee's were hanging around in the restroom. I could never understand why a person would want to hang around in a restroom when they could be sitting in a booth. My employer's solution; it was winter time and extremely cold outside, so he turned the heat off in the restrooms.

Guess what? No more problems with employees hanging around in the restrooms!

In one place where I worked a new waitress came to work on a weekend and everyone thought that it was strange that a new person would be trained on a busy weekend.

Laws were different many years ago. Nowadays, people would never legally get away with what our employer had done.

Not only was a small tape recorder hidden under the counter where the employees had a habit of sitting, but the new waitress was a spy for our employer.

She gave a bad report on everyone, except me. I was the youngest person there and I was the only person she gave a good report on.

The hidden tape recorder? Well, our employer sure got an earful! The employee's were talking about him and they had nothing good to say about him.

Sometimes habits are hard to break, unless of course, we are forced into breaking our habits.

Many years ago, a dollar would go a long way. Coffee could be bought for 10¢ a cup, with no free refills. Free refills were never heard of back then. I can remember hamburgers being 49¢ and these were big hamburgers and hot dogs were 25¢ each.

Every Saturday night it became a habit for a man to come into the restaurant with a hundred dollar bill. Since things were so cheap back then, and banks were not open on Saturdays, it was difficult for the restaurant to give this man change.

One Saturday night, my employer was there and he was ready for the man with the hundred dollar bill.

When the man came in with the hundred dollar bill, my employer gave the man rolls of coins and I mean this man's change were all rolls of coins! Needless to say, this forced the man into breaking his habit.

In one restaurant, I was given a key to the front door one night so that I could let myself in the restaurant the next morning at 6:00AM to start doing the prep. In case you don't know what prep is; it is getting the food prepared.

This was a buffet style of restaurant and I was working on cold bar prep, which included cutting onions, tomatoes, etc. When the restaurant opened at 11:00AM, I would have all of the prep done and the cold bar completely set up and then I would switch over to being a waitress.

However, apparently one manager was not told of the arrangement, because he arrived at 8:00AM and he thought it was strange to see a car parked near the back door. Very carefully he sneaked in the front door and was looking around for a possible burglar. When he got to the back of the restaurant, he heard noises. We both got a big scare and a big laugh.

One day I cleaned a table off when some people left and about a half an hour later the people came back. The woman said she left her false teeth on the table wrapped in a napkin. I never saw any false teeth and I was sure I would have known if I picked up a napkin and her false teeth were wrapped in the napkin.

It sure was a sight to see the woman go through the trash looking for her false teeth! The restaurant was busy, so no one had time to help her look through the trash.

The next day, this woman called the restaurant and said she found her false teeth wrapped in a napkin, in her purse.

A similar situation happened to a young girl I knew who was at that time wearing an appliance in her mouth. The appliance was never found, however.

Have you ever worked in a situation where there was someone who gossips a lot? I have worked in that situation, but it was more than one person in the work place who gossiped and "bad mouthed" the other employees.

This really does a lot of damage to the place of business.

Now imagine if you were a gossip and while you are doing the gossiping the person who you are talking about was standing behind you.

Without the person's knowledge, I walked up to the person and stood behind her while she was talking about me to someone. I never said a word, just stood there.

Imagine how foolish she felt when she realized I was standing there.

In some restaurants in our area, something special is done for a customer's birthday.

One night, an employee came in as a customer on his birthday. We clapped our hands as we were walking to where he was sitting, then we put a birthday cake in front of him and we sang the special birthday song.

This young man had been drinking alcohol and he got so embarrassed with everyone around him singing and clapping their hands that he accidentally put his entire face in the birthday cake.

In one restaurant where I worked, the accountant was a husband and wife team. These people came into the restaurant every morning, so they got to know all of us quite well.

I always looked forward to their visits, because we joked a lot!

One day the man brought in a large roll of duct tape and put it on the end of the table. When I asked him what the duct tape was for, he promptly told me it was to tape my mouth shut because I talked too much.

A few minutes later when he "wasn't looking" I grabbed the duct tape and hit it.

We laughed and joked about it and I gave the duct tape back to him when he left.

To the same couple, I played another joke, but I had to enlist the help of the manager.

In this restaurant there was a large metal box right outside of the side door which held bags of ice. We sold the bags of ice and we also would use the bags of ice in the restaurant.

One morning when this couple came into the restaurant, I got the key from the cash register and went out the side door to get a bag of ice.

Before I actually got the ice, I picked up the pay telephone that was beside the big metal ice box and called the restaurant.

Since the manager was in on the joke, she answered the phone then called the husband to the phone. When he came to the phone and said "hello," I asked him, "Do you know where your waitress is?" I could hear he was trying hard not to laugh when he said, "I don't know and I don't care," and I said, "Oh, okay! See ya, bye." Then I walked back into the restaurant with a bag of ice.

The husband was sitting facing the door that I came into and I could see his face was red, his shoulders were going up and down and he was trying so hard not to burst out laughing. His poor wife was sitting there with her back to the side door where I came in and she was laughing, but yet she appeared to not know what actually happened, but yet she knew whatever it was, it was funny.

Another time when I was working in a buffet restaurant, I had to again enlist the manager's help to play a joke on another manager.

I went to the pay phone and called the other manager. Then I asked the manager, "Do you know where your hot bar person is?", since I was taking care of the hot food on the food bar that day.

The manager tried not to laugh and he said, "I don't know, but she better get back to work." When I walked past the office door, his face was red and he was laughing.

When I was working the graveyard shift one night, the cook got upset over something and he walked out of the restaurant and went home. Around 2:00AM, we got a sudden rush and there were only two servers working.

The other server ran to the kitchen and cooked while I took the orders, served the food and took the people's money at the cash register.

When things slowed up, the server who was cooking discovered she had three extra hamburger patties cooked. It was about then that a man came in the door who had ordered three hamburgers to go and none of his hamburgers had the hamburger patties inside the buns.

People in our area who worked the grave yard shift know that strange things happen on the night of the full moon. Servers do not like to work weekends on the grave yard shift when the full moon comes on the weekend.

I was told that one woman who worked in a tavern said that she always knew when it was a full moon without looking outside by the customers who came through the door. Some people never came in the tavern unless it was a full moon.

One evening I was working and the entire evening was strange. Customers were even stranger that entire night.

When one of the manager's wives came in, employees were telling her about the crazy night so far since she also worked there as a manager and it wasn't even midnight yet.

I then said that as strange as the whole evening had been so far, there must be a full moon, to which she replied, "There is a full moon tonight!"

In one buffet restaurant, a young girl was working one day. She worked on the cold bar and I worked on the hot bar. She and I were about the same height, same weight, same color hair and eyes and we both had our hair in a ponytail, but she was in her twenty's and I was in my early fifty's.

Now, we all know as a person gets older, their eye sight changes. Let's face it, people's eye sight is just not what it is when they were younger.

One day as I came out with hot food to fill the hot bar, the young girl was standing at the cold bar filling up the cold bar with cold food.

This young girl was talking to an elderly lady. The elderly lady turned around and saw me, turned and looked at the young girl, looked at me, then looked at the young girl and with a shocked look on her face and a surprised tone of voice blurted out, "Oh twins!"

I will never forget the very first dispute I ever witnessed between a waitress and a customer.

I was sixteen and was just starting my career as a restaurant worker. Many years ago every restaurant had a glass sugar bowl on every table.

One evening the waitress who was working on the opposite end of the restaurant, (there were only two of us working that night), got into a dispute with a man customer. It was getting louder, and they were each extremely angry with the other one. The problem? He wanted her to fill the sugar bowl because he said it was half empty and she insisted it was not half empty, but it was half full.

When I was working in one restaurant, sometimes I worked past midnight until the bar crowd left. The restaurant did not serve alcohol, but these were people who came in after the local bars closed. These people were usually drunk and we never knew what to expect.

One time a woman got up on her table and danced.

Another time a woman was going back and forth dancing on the long counter. People were pulling their coffee and food off the counter so that she wouldn't step in it.

Another time yet, a man found a shopping cart in the parking lot from a local grocery store. In our area, we call the baskets with wheels that people use in stores shopping carts. I know when I lived down south they were called buggies.

This man brought the shopping cart into the restaurant and his wife climbed into the cart and he pushed the cart with his wife in it around the restaurants dining room. They even went behind the counter and when they passed the pie case, she yelled out that she wanted a certain piece of pie and her husband stopped the cart, she reached in the pie case and took the piece of pie, he grabbed a clean fork that was near him and gave the fork to her, then he started pushing the cart with his wife sitting in the cart eating the pie.

The entire place was in an uproar with laughter and I had tears going down my face from laughing so hard.

One night a couple came into the restaurant and I was their waitress.

It appeared that there was a problem between them because the man was speaking in angry tones, then he would bang his fist on the table and yell things like, "If you don't start behaving yourself, I'm going to send you out to the car!" Finally, I went over to them and told them to please go outside if they are going to argue.

Imagine my surprise when I discovered that he was extremely angry at an imaginary friend! This couple had just been evicted from a local bar because he was yelling and banging his fist on a table at his imaginary friend.

It really amazes me how some people ask strange questions, such as: "What is this, mashed potatoes?" or "Is this spaghetti?"

One question that I find especially amusing is, "Do you have a restroom?" I often wonder what people's reaction would be if I would say to them that we have no restroom or the restroom is in the little wooden building out back.

A new fad was just coming out for the young people to wear baggy pants about ten sizes to large.

One young man I worked with wore such pants to work one day, but only one day.

The day he wore those baggy pants, he bent over the counter to talk to someone and we saw you know what from behind.

The cashier grabbed a salt shaker and without touching him, poured salt down the back of his pants. Like I said, he never wore those baggy pants again.

One day, several women came in to eat and they had several small children with them.

The one mother was talking and waving her hands when she knocked over her soda.

Imagine how embarrassed she was when her daughter told me that it was her mommy that knocked the soda over. By the way, the little girl had a happy look on her face when she told me.

Do you know what hotcakes are? Some people call them pancakes, or flapjacks, or even griddle cakes. Whatever you call them, have you ever seen a person eat ketchup on them?

I thought that was something that was done only in the comic strips until I actually saw a man eat them that way.

One day, an employee went up to a manger and slapped him on the back while joking and laughing with him.

Imagine the manager's surprise when he found out that when the employee had slapped him on the back the employee had actually put a sign on the manager's back that read, "I am going crazy."

One day my employer went out the side door which had a large glass window in it. Suddenly the temptation got too much for me. I ran to the door, locked the door and when he tried to get back in the door, I stood there and waved at him.

One day it "rained" pennies in the restaurant. I picked up a total of 0.36¢. Young people are amused when I bend over and pick up a penny, but my logic is that pennies add up.

To eat a cheeseburger with bacon on it is a very popular item in our local area. I will never forget the first time I ever heard of bacon on a cheeseburger.

A man came into the restaurant and ordered a cheeseburger with bacon on it and me; being a teenager and I laughed a lot anyway, burst out laughing because I thought the man was joking.

This man looked at me as if I had gone crazy, because he was from California and a bacon cheeseburger was a very popular food item there. He didn't realize that a bacon cheeseburger was unheard of on the east coast.

I must admit, now, a bacon cheeseburger is one of my favorite food items.

One day I was standing in the back of the restaurant and when the manager walked out of the dish room, I had a question for him.

While we were talking, a funny look came across his face. He kept looking at his feet, then at me.

When I looked towards the floor, I understood the strange embarrassed look on his face. His pants had fallen down to his feet!

I burst out laughing until I was crying and I had to lean against something so that I would not collapse to the floor laughing. I had such an uncontrollable laugh that even though I was in the back of the restaurant customers could hear me laughing out front of the restaurant.

The women in the prep area looked to see what was so funny then, they started laughing too.

I must admit, I will never forget the look on the manager's face, because at that moment, the look on his face was priceless.

I have worked with a midget in the past. Many people think she is a small child, even though she was in her early twenty's.

One night when she was working in a restaurant, a little boy walked up to her and he got a shocked look on his face. Being about five or six years old, the little boy said to the midget, "Do you work here?" She replied, she did, and the little boy said, "But you're so little!" and the little boy's father got really embarrassed.

Many times over the years when people see this girl working when children are in school, people will ask her why she's not in school and they quickly mention the child labor laws.

One time this little midget girl went to a buffet restaurant with her mother, grandmother and her older sister.

The cashier thought the older sister was the younger sister's mother. The older sister got really upset saying that she didn't think she looked that old.

Her mother tried to calm the older girl by saying that some girls do have babies when they are quite young and the younger girl is so small that people mistake the younger sister for being around twelve.

When the four of them had gotten a plate of food and sat down together, the younger sister got a devilish look on her face and she snickered as she said, that while the four of them were in line, she should have very loudly said to her older sister, "Mommy, I need to go the bathroom!"

I was working in the bakery section of a restaurant. When I got there that morning I was given a list of things to do.

However, I was going to take a week's vacation the following week and I didn't realize how badly I needed that vacation until it was pointed out to me that instead of putting frosting on the brownies, I had put frosting on the fudge.

There was an older lady who worked in the restaurant I was working in.

One evening she had three young men come in and the one young man thought he was so smart. He wanted to show off for his two friends.

The older lady, who was their waitress, heard the one young man say to his two friends, "Watch how I am going to upset our waitress". What this young man didn't know was that no one ever got anything over on this lady.

When the lady brought their food, she asked if there was anything she could get them?

The show off looked at her and said he wanted a vanilla ice cream, also.

Since the ice cream freezer was directly behind her, the lady turned around and scooped out his vanilla ice cream and holding the scoop in her hand with the ice cream still the in scoop, she asked the young man where he wanted his ice cream?

The young man looked at his two friends and snickered and he said, "I want my ice cream there," and pointed to his hamburger.

Much to his horror and his friend's amusement the lady waitress dropped the scoop of ice cream on top of his hamburger. She then asked him if there was anything else she could get him and he stuttered "No."

Another night, a terrible ruckus was heard in the men's room. It was discovered that there were two men fist fighting in the men's room.

The older lady, who was a waitress, knew exactly how to stop the men from fighting. She told us to grab a bucket of ice with some water in it and bring it to her.

When someone brought her the bucket of ice water, someone held the men's room door wide open while she threw the bucket of ice water on the two fighting men.

What a shock to the two men! They were also shocked to see a woman standing inside the men's room.

Then the older waitress yelled for them to take their fight outside.

Neither man said a word, but both of them walked out the front door, each man got into their own car and left without saying a single word.

In a buffet restaurant, the wait staff has a tendency to ask the question, "Would you like to keep your spoon and fork?" when the server is collecting the dirty dishes and eating utensils. A lot of people like to keep their spoon or fork for dessert.

One time a server asked a woman if she wanted to keep her spoon and fork and the woman said, "No thank you, we have plenty at home!"

One time I asked a woman if she wanted to keep her spoon or fork and the woman's eyes got big and she asked me, "Do you mean we can keep the eating utensils?"

When I was young I never thought about how certain brands of pies were only made in our area of the country.

One day some customers asked me who bakes the restaurant's pies (I will make up the name of a pie here, since I do not want to mention a specific brand of pie). I told them Mrs. Jones baked the pie and they asked me who was Mrs. Jones and I, and not knowing they had never heard of Mrs. Jones brand of pie, I replied to them, "She's the lady who married Mr. Jones."

There was one hostess that had a habit of being five minutes late, every day. One day we saw her drive into the parking lot and park her car.

We gathered near the front door. Imagine the surprised look on her face when she walked in the front door and there were six of us standing there clapping our hands.

I have heard of malt vinegar, and I have seen malt vinegar on the shelves in grocery stores, but I had never smelled it. One day I walked up to a table and a terrible odor hit my nose I was so sure that someone had their shoes off and their feet smelled horrible.

Imagine my surprise when I realized no one had the shoes off but the horrible odor was the malt vinegar!

I still cannot understand how someone can put something in their mouth that smells like a person's smelly feet!"

One night a couple came into the restaurant and she knew what she wanted to eat, so she told me her order. However, the man didn't know what he wanted to eat and it was about ten minutes later when he finally decided what he wanted. He gave me his order and apparently he forgot that I had already taken her food order.

When he realized I already knew what she wanted to eat, he got a shocked look on his face and he asked her how I knew what she wanted to eat.

I saw a perfect opportunity to play a joke on the man that I had never met.

I told him that I'm a mind reader and he had better be careful what he was thinking about the woman he was with or I would tell her exactly what he was thinking.

This poor man! He sat there with his mouth hanging open and a shocked look on his face, looking back and forth from the woman to me.

Suddenly he said "Okay, okay! I won't think anymore!" Then he turned his back to me and looked out the window.

A man was hired as a cook and he had told the manager he didn't know how to cook before he was hired. One day, somehow, he had the oven on fire and I mean there were actual flames inside the oven! I still don't know how he did that!

One day I was working on cold bar prep, which meant I was preparing the cold food for the cold bar buffet.

Two managers came walking through carrying a door between them. I realized they were going to replace the door on the men's room, which somehow had gotten damaged.

Temptation got the best of me. I just had to say, "Oh, who won the door prize?"

The two managers suddenly stopped walking because they were laughing so hard and one of them said, "You did, Helen, you won the door prize!"

When I was still in my teen years and working in a restaurant about five or six in the morning, several men came in to eat breakfast.

One man put sugar in his coffee and salt on his eggs. Shortly after that, he called me over to the table. Someone had put sugar in the salt shaker and salt in the sugar bowl.

Much to my delight, I found out a few years later, who had made the switch.

I was a newlywed and my husband and I moved into a mobile home park.

When we met our new neighbors and the young man found out I worked at the restaurant he started laughing and bragging about how he had switched the salt & sugar a few years before.

He really thought I was joking at first when I told him I was his waitress at that time. Now I know who did it!

At another restaurant, I was dipping ice cream when the lid to the tub of ice cream fell to the bottom of the freezer. When I tried to reach the lid I almost fell into the freezer head fist.

I kept laughing about what a funny sight that would have been, my head in the bottom of the ice cream freezer and my feet towards the ceiling.

One tiny girl I know, who is 4'9" tall, was cleaning a tall sink one day and she almost fell in head first and she thought that she might have to be rescued because she was hanging over the sink and her feet weren't even touching the floor. She was really embarrassed, but she finally got herself off the side of the sink.

I had a picture in my mind of her falling into the sink and then peeking out to see if anyone was looking before she climbed out.

In one restaurant, suddenly it became a problem that employees kept asking for another employee's phone number to request someone to cover their shift. One manager decided to hang everyone's phone numbers on the billboard.

A mother and daughter were working at the restaurant together, and there was also a new dishwasher that the mother was not too impressed with.

One night, the phone rang at home, and the mother answered. The caller asked for the daughter and when the caller gave his name, the mother immediately recognized the dishwasher's name.

The mother asked if he knew who he was talking to and he said, "Yes, her mother", and then the mother asked if he knew who the mother was.

There was complete silence on the other end of the phone and then he stammered a "No", to which the mother told him that she also worked at the restaurant.

The mother could just picture in her mind the look on his face as she identified herself and he quickly got off the phone and when the mother hung up her phone she stood there and laughed. If only the mother could have seen the look on his face! He had no idea when he called that the mother worked at the restaurant, also.

One night as part of a tip, I received a one dollar bill with scotch tape on it. I thought nothing of it, as I had received money with scotch tape on it before.

When I left work, I made a stop at a local store.

When I gave the cashier the one dollar bill with the scotch tape on it, she gave me the dollar bill back and told me she could not accept the money.

I was shocked, so I asked her when the store had stopped accepting cash. She told me she could not accept that dollar bill because the serial numbers on both halves were different. Sure enough, when I looked, she was correct. The two pieces of money were a perfect fit.

The pay phone was located in a very small hallway, between the restrooms and the restaurants office.

One night a man tried to use the pay phone and suddenly there was a busy rush on people going to the restrooms and people going back and forth to the office and all of this created a lot of noise.

Suddenly, the man on the pay phone yelled, "Hey what is this, Grand Central Station?"

In one family, the mother was working in a doctor's office and the oldest daughter was working in a restaurant.

One night, the daughter left home to make a quick stop at a local mom and pop type of store. Just when she left, the home phone rang and the mother answered it.

It was the manager of the restaurant where the daughter worked. The manager was so sure he was talking to the daughter and she was playing a joke on him saying she was really her mother. The mother had a good time trying to convince the manager she was not her daughter. The manager and the mother really had a good laugh.

Shortly after they hung up the phone, the daughter walked in the front door. The mother and daughter had a good laugh over it, and then the daughter retuned the manager's phone call.

The manager and the daughter enjoyed a good laugh over the whole mix up and about two months later, the mother quit her job at the doctor's off and went to work at the restaurant where her daughter worked!

In another restaurant where I worked, I usually saw an adult couple come in with their son.

One day, the son came with a friend. I made a casual comment about his parents not being with them in which he quickly replied, "This is my parents favorite restaurant, so please don't tell them you saw us here without them!"

One day a manager came into the restaurant with his family to eat.

I walked up to the manager and said, "I just had some people get up and leave." He got a serious look on his face and he said, "Why did they leave?" I started laughing and I said, "Because they were done eating!"

A young man was hired to carve meat in a buffet restaurant.

I must admit, I have to question what the young man ever ate.

He was told to get another ham. He went to the food warmer to pull the ham out. This young man asked someone near him "Is this the ham?" And the funny reply came, "No it's turkey!" Sensing the man was teasing, the young man asked someone else "Is this ham?" and this person who likes to joke a lot said, "No it's steak," so being confused, the young man yelled, "Hey, where's the ham?" What did the young man already have in his hands? Why, ham, of course!

People often say to me that a certain food item is good, then just for conversation they will ask me if I cooked it. My silly reply? "No, I didn't cook it. If I cooked it you would not want it. I must confess though, that my cooking is getting better and I know my cooking is getting better because my first one hundred husbands are six feet under, but my last twelve husbands have survived my cooking!" That always brings a good laugh.

People, all the time mistake me for being at least fifteen years younger, so I hope I can continue to fool people like that.

One day, though, a man must have had a terrible shock. He was behind me and he walked up to me and said, "Miss," and when I turned around, he got a strange look on his face and he jumped backward several times.

He said from behind, he thought I was about seventeen. I didn't mind that at all, but he sure must have been shocked again. When I told him I was fifty four, he looked shocked and jumped backwards several times again.

An older lady I worked with years ago had a very real phobia of closed in places. I didn't realize how much so until several things happened.

One night our employer went to lock the restaurant's front doors, since it was Christmas Eve and the restaurant was closing for Christmas.

The older lady saw him locking the front doors and she ran so fast out of one of the front doors that she almost knocked our employer down the steps.

Another time her mechanic came to the restaurant to pick up her car to do some repair work on it. This lady lived about a half mile up the highway but it was a busy highway and it was after midnight when she got off work, so someone took her home.

This lady had such a phobia of closed in places, that she just had to travel the half mile home in this person's car with the car door part way open, just enough so that she could put her toes out the car door.

One night just before leaving work as I gave the manager all my credit card slips. I made a comment about all the credit cards that were used.

My employer was also in the office. He said it was a good thing I didn't receive any of the new metal credit cards because we were not yet equipped for the new credit cards.

I looked at him, for I thought for sure that he must have been joking. Metal credit cards? He appeared to be serious enough, though. I said, "You're kidding, metal credit cards?"

He went on to explain that a new attachment for the computers were due in any day.

I asked, "But why metal credit cards?" He said "the plastic credit cards break too easily."

I kept looking at him and I kept thinking he must be joking, but he still appeared to be serious, so I said to him that at first I thought he was joking about the metal credit cards. Then the manager said, my employer was joking, and the three of us had a good hearty laugh.

One morning the hostess called the manager to the phone because someone wanted to make a reservation for thirty people.

While the manager was talking on the phone, a server who was talking on his cell phone, walked closer to the manager.

That's when the manager realized he was talking to the server on the server's cell phone that was playing a joke on the manager.

One night I received a bigger tip because the man said, I looked real thin and I probably needed the money to buy food.

I worked with a woman from England. One day, some people from England came into the restaurant.

Much to her delight, they were from her home town in England, and they knew her brother and other family members who still lived in her home town in England. It was truly amazing!

One night a couple and their ten year old daughter came into the restaurant.

What a pleasant surprise for me! They recognized me from another restaurant ten years before! I could not imagine anyone would recognize me or ever remember me after ten years!

They faxed a nice letter about me to the franchise home office and the franchise home office sent me a nice letter with a service pin to wear.

In one restaurant, there were two Helen's and one Ellen.

When two or all three of us were working at the same time, and someone called Helen or Ellen, then all of us would answer.

In one restaurant, the new cook was burning all the food he cooked, while he was saying that he didn't know why they had put him to cooking because he told them before he was hired the he didn't know how to cook.

One day I was working with a manager who had a new shirt on. Much to everyone's surprise, when the evening manager arrived at work, he also had a new shirt on and it was identical to the new shirt the daytime manager had on. The two managers even had on the same color pants!

I enjoy walking to the post office when the weather permits. My walk is between four and a half to five miles round trip.

It amazes me how many people recognize me as "the walker", when they see me working in a restaurant or anywhere else.

I make a lot of my earrings by buying fancy buttons and I glue the backs on them. I have one set of buttons with backs glued on them and my earrings are a smiley face. Every time I wear these earrings, I always receive compliments on them. I always thought I would never see another pair of earrings that look exactly like mine.

One night a young girl came into the restaurant with earrings exactly like my smiley face earrings. She told me she buys buttons and glues backs on them also. I no longer have an only set of smiley face earrings.

Another time, a couple came into the restaurant and they wanted to know where I purchased my smiley face earrings because they wanted to purchase a smiley face set of earrings for someone. I was certainly amused.

There were two couples that came into the restaurant together. When the food came, for some reason one man decided to shake the ketchup bottle. When the man attempted to shake the ketchup, the lid flew off and ketchup flew out of the bottle and he had ketchup on the side of his face and neck. It is very understandable why this man sat there with a stunned look on his face.

Another time, someone I know was sitting in a booth with his wife. A woman was sitting directly behind my friend, when he felt something hit the back of his head and that is when the woman in the next booth was very embarrassed. For some reason, she decided to shake her steak sauce bottle, and the lid went flying through the air and my friend had steak sauce in his hair and on his neck. My friend and his wife were strangers to the two people sitting directly behind my friend.

One night I walked past a man sitting with his family. Much to my amusement, he was licking the handle to his fork. I have never seen anyone lick a fork handle before! I heard of finger licking good, but this was the first time I ever heard of fork licking good.

In one restaurant, we were required to wear neckties. One evening, eight people came in together. Everyone was surprised that the restaurant's employees were wearing the exact same necktie as one of the men in their party of people.

The man said he got his necktie at the beach. I said, "I really don't think we got ours at the beach", to which he replied by flicking his necktie and said, "I bet your necktie is not pure silk", and I replied "Probably not, but someone may come to you and ask a question because they will think you work here." Next time I walked past their table, the man had taken his necktie off.

One new employee did not know I wore short hair wigs in the winter. In order to do this, I must pile my long hair up under the wig.

Being classified as a senior citizen, I never am upset over being mistaken for a much younger person. It's like wearing a hat; my head is warmer, so I'm warmer.

One day I was in the dish room leaving some dirty dishes when the new employee turned around and saw the back of me. This young man thought he was looking at a new employee and he thought that new employee was about seventeen years old, and he couldn't remember seeing this new person around high school, so he wanted to meet this "new chick." Imagine his surprise when I turned around and he saw me!

Honestly, it's okay to mistake me for a teenager, even if it's from behind!

One day a woman walked into a buffet restaurant and she wanted to take food out. She was given a box to fill with food. The box was square and it had a hinged lid. She filled the box and the lid with food, and then she complained that this was the strangest take out box that she had ever seen because if she lifted the lid to close the box, the food from the lid would fall on top of the food that was in the bottom part of the box.

There was a dessert called chocolate wow, and believe me, there was a reason why the word wow was in the name of the dessert. More than one person took their first bite, and said, "Wow."

One day I saw a lady customer accidently knock over a glass of ice water. The ice water went directly on the lap of a man sitting with her. I was expecting the man to get upset but he didn't. I knew he had to be embarrassed to get up and walk out when he was done eating because the water had not gone on his shirt, but the water had gone on his lap.

The ice tea brewer was broken, so we had no ice tea, which was a popular beverage. One man came into the restaurant by himself, and he wanted ice tea. When I explained that we had no ice tea, he said, "Oh no! Everywhere I have been this morning, there has been something wrong!" I looked at him and said, "This had not been a good day for you, has it?" He replied, "It sure hasn't been a good day!" As he was getting ready to leave after paying his food bill, I thanked him for coming and I told him that I hoped the rest of his day will go well. He said, "So do I!"

One evening a young couple came into the restaurant with two small boys, the oldest boy around four years old and the youngest sat in a highchair. The little boy in the highchair kept crying and his older brother turned to his dad and said, "I never cried when I was little, did I, Dad?" Then the boy turned to me and said, "And I didn't pull hair, either!"

A couple came into the restaurant and the husband ordered a very rare steak. He said throw the steak on the grill and immediately flip the steak, and quickly put the steak on a plate for him. His wife said he likes his steak still mooing, in which I replied that as long as it didn't moo, then it was okay, because if his steak moos, then I was heading for the door.

April Fool! April first is known as April Fools' Day and people like to play jokes on other people.

One customer who had to be in his fifties told me a funny, but true story.

His grandmother was someone who always liked to play jokes on people, so it just seemed natural for her to marry on April first. On her wedding day, very few people were there, because they thought it was another one of her jokes.

Even more strange was that many years later, her husband was buried on April first.

Chapter Two

Other Interesting Things

These things you may not find funny, but you will certainly enjoy anyway.

No person's name or restaurants name is given to protect those who give us interesting thing to read about.

WHEN I LIVED in South Carolina, I had a five day stay in a local hospital.

My one roommate worked in a local restaurant.

She told me she always knew during breakfast which customers were from the South and which customers were from the North. How? Easy! The people who ate grits with their breakfast were from the South and those who ate hash brown potatoes were from the North.

Back in the 1960's, a waitress had somehow dropped her money, which was all coins, in the ladies room toilet. She couldn't afford to lose a whole night's worth of tips, so she scooped the coins out of the toilet with her hand.

One night a young teenage couple came into the restaurant with only $2.00 between them, so they ordered one soda with two straws. They sat there talking and laughing and really enjoying each other's company. It really was a nice scene.

In restaurants where alcohol is served, we must ask for an ID to verify that a person is at least twenty one years old. I was really impressed when I looked at one woman's picture ID.

She had lost a lot of weight and I had to take a second and third look to make sure it was really her on her ID.

One night in the restaurant where I was working at was an unusually funny night. No joking! Eight funny things happened in one eight hour shift. I wish I could remember everything that happened that night. I was sore from laughing that night.

The other woman I was working with that night saw nothing funny and she got upset over everything and her face turned a bright red because her blood pressure kept going up. I was really concerned for her, but yet I kept laughing about everything.

Normally, there is nothing funny about a person getting sick to their stomach, but so far that night, it had been so crazy in there, I found the following to be funny.

Two young couples came to the cash register to pay their bill. All of a sudden the five of us heard a strange noise, so we looked in the direction of which the sound came from.

There was a long haired man lying in the booth, but his finger tips were bouncing around on the tabletop. When his hand touched some napkins, he grabbed the napkins then his hand disappeared. The whole scene was funny and even the two couples were snickering.

The two men went back to check on the man, and when they came back, they announced, that the man was sick. All five of us started laughing.

I apologized to them for I was hanging over the cash register crying from laughing so hard, and I told them that I don't usually laugh about a person's misfortune, but the entire night had so far been positively hilarious.

I went into the kitchen where the manager was cooking and I tried to tell her about the man being sick but because I kept thinking about how funny it looked to see the man's hand bounce on the table, and the night has been so funny up to that moment, all I could do was laugh.

The manager started laughing, but she had no idea why she was laughing. She was laughing because I was laughing.

After four attempts, I finally was able to tell her when she was in the office, and oh, if only you could have seen her face! She was laughing, and I told her finally why I was laughing and her face got serious, and she said to me, "You are laughing about that?" Like I said, though, usually I don't laugh about things like that but the entire night had been so funny.

This poor man walked out the front door of the restaurant so I thought that he went home. I think he was sick because he had been in a local bar and he had been drinking too much alcohol. What I didn't know was that he went to the back door of the restaurant and laid on the ground.

Now, there is nothing funny about that, but, however, we had a teenager washing dishes that night. This teenage dishwasher went outside the back door, and saw that poor man laying on the ground and this teenager, who was going to change the mop head on the mop to scrub the kitchen floor, put the new mop head on his own head and started jumping around and making noises.

That poor man on the ground moaned and looked at the dishwasher as if the dishwasher was crazy.

One night I was standing behind the restaurants counter. I started thinking about something funny and I started to snicker.

Much to my horror, a man sitting at the counter was insulted because I snickered, because right at the moment I snickered, a man at the cash register was purchasing medicine for his heartburn and the man sitting at the counter thought I was snickering because the man at the cash register had heartburn.

One day during lunch in a buffet restaurant where I was working, a group of young people came in to eat lunch. They paid for their buffet, got plates, filled their plates, and then sat down to eat. That's when one of the young girls complained to me that she could not find anything she liked on the buffet and she wanted her money back.

I was shocked! It was a big buffet and to find nothing to eat was not possible!

As her money was being returned to her, I was thinking that she probably didn't have the money to spare to eat out, so that was probably her way of being with her friends but yet not have to spend her money.

There was a man who started to come in for breakfast on the weekends at a buffet restaurant where I was working.

He was an older man, in poor physical condition, not the most intelligent man and I felt sorry for him.

Every time he came in he used his walker and I got plates and walked him through the buffet getting his food for him and helping him to get a place to sit.

I assumed this man was very lonely and probably not many people wanted to be near him because he smelled so badly.

This man decided he was in love with me and even though I felt sorry for him and I was willing to help him in any way I could, I was not in love with him.

This man would proclaim loudly that he loved me. One day, it got busy during breakfast and he yelled way across the restaurant that he loved me. On the third yell, everyone was looking at me as if wondering what was going on between him and me.

I walked up to him and I tried in a nice way to tell him not to do that, and what happened next, I felt a mixture of shock, horror and embarrassment. He started sobbing and I mean really sobbing! His head was on his arms which were on the table, and he was really sobbing from deep inside.

I didn't know what to do so I tried to comfort him while explaining that I didn't want him to yell out any more that he loved me.

Many years ago when music boxes were on every table, a man came into the restaurant and showed us how to make the counter top music boxes play music without putting any money in. I would never recommend this to anyone because now that I'm older, I realize what a dangerous thing we were doing. I must admit, though, that we enjoyed music all night without paying any money.

There was an elderly man who was a regular customer. He was lonely and he grew up as a foster child. We enjoyed having him come in every day as much as he enjoyed coming in.

This man never really knew his actual birthday or his actual age. This sounds strange today, but years ago things were much different. This man picked a date and said that was his birthday.

One year we decided to do something special for his "birthday." Someone had brought a small package of cupcakes and a birthday candle into the restaurant. When this man came in, we put the candle on the cupcake and we sang happy birthday to him.

All of us were surprised to see him crying. He told us this was the very first birthday cake he ever had.

It really amazes me how a person can drink alcohol until they are sick.

One night I was working at a wedding reception when I saw a woman get sick, her husband grabbed a cloth napkin, and she was getting sick in the cloth napkin. Immediately after that, she got up and started dancing. I assumed she felt better after getting sick.

I didn't feel so well when her husband wanted me to take the cloth napkin away because his wife "spilled something on it."

Since I saw what happened I thought, "Yeah, she spilled something alright. She spilled something from her stomach!"

I said I would be right back to get the cloth napkin. I went into the kitchen, got a takeout box, took the take out box to the husband, let him put the cloth napkin in the takeout box, then, I threw the box with the cloth napkin in it, in the trash.

There was an older man, his wife, and teenage daughter who used to come into the restaurant.

They rarely took baths or showers. We all knew it because of the odors.

One day the man came into the restaurant by himself. He yelled to our employer across the restaurant that he was really tired because he had just taken his monthly bath and his monthly bath always tires him out.

All of us believed him.

An elderly man and his wife were regular customers, and we really enjoyed their company.

One day they got into their car and instead of putting his foot on the brake, he put his foot on the gas pedal. Disaster hit! He ran the car into the restaurant.

A man was sitting near the door when the car ran into the restaurant and the car came through the door. The sitting man went straight up into the air and back down into his seat and the bowl of soup he was eating was upside down on his head.

The elderly man and his wife were terribly upset, but everyone tried to assure them everything was okay and no one was hurt.

I was working midnight to 8:00AM on the weekends.

One morning a few young people came in together. Thy told us that they travel from night club to night club to dance. They had no interest in drinking alcohol, but they only wanted to dance. One young girl gave us a demonstration on how to dance.

Now imagine, about thirty five years later, I met this same girl again only this time she was more mature and had no interest in going to night clubs to dance anymore. This woman came to work where I was working. She and I started talking one day and we realized it was her that I met about thirty five years ago in a different restaurant than the restaurant we were working in at that time.

There was an artist that came into the restaurant every night and every night he would turn his paper placemat over to where there was a plain white side.

This artist would then pick out someone and draw that person on his placemat.

One night his drawing became a problem when one man sitting at the counter became aware that the artist was drawing his picture. This man jumped up from his seat at the counter, grabbed the artist and was ready to hit the artist when all the servers who were working that night came to the artist rescue.

The man had a wife in another state that was looking for him and this man thought the artist may have been a private detective that his wife hired to look for him.

Why do people want to drink until they are sick?

Many times when I stayed past midnight on the weekends to work until the bar crowd left I would see people get sick because of the alcohol they had consumed.

One time a man got sick on his breakfast while sitting at the counter.

Another time a man got up from the counter and started walking towards the restrooms and while he was walking towards the restroom he was getting sick. A woman customer sitting in a booth saw him, and she got a sick look on her face.

One time after a man left a bar, he came into the restaurant to eat. This man fell to sleep with his head in the hotcakes on his plate and he had already put syrup on his hotcakes.

These days, lights hanging from the ceiling are made of lightweight material, but years ago that was not the case.

One late afternoon I was standing next to the cashier and I was telling her something.

Much to her disbelief I suddenly said, "You won't believe what I just saw", and she said, "What did you just see?"

I told her the entire bottom half of the heavy glass lamp that was hanging from the ceiling just broke, fell, and hit the top of a man's head that was sitting in a booth.

She thought I was joking at first, but I guess the look on my face said I wasn't joking.

She and I checked on the man, but in spite of being dazed and a small cut on his bald head, he was fine.

Every time I was pregnant I started "showing" immediately. Always at two and a half months. I could not wear my own clothes. I was not rushing things, but I honestly could not wear my own clothes at two and a half months.

I was about two months pregnant and just one week away from my first doctor's appointment.

Two middle age couples came into the restaurant and when they saw me they knew I was pregnant by looking at me and these four people were total strangers to me.

At one work place, a young man had just graduated from a military boot camp.

At my other work place, a woman and a girl about twenty years old came in.

They told me the woman's son had just graduated from a military boot camp and the young girl around twenty years old was the young man's girlfriend. Much to all of our amazement, I knew the young man they were talking about, because I had worked with the young man at my other work place and I had seen him just a few days before when he came into the other work place in his dress uniform.

A relative of mine came to work at the same restaurant where I was working.

A man with whom we were working with developed a crush on this relative of mine, but she wasn't interested in him.

To make a long story short, things had advanced to where I had a fear of this girl being kidnapped. I had even told this young girl to be very, very careful when she went home after dark or if she went anywhere after dark. I am not afraid of anyone, no matter how big or how mean they are. I will back down from a dispute quickly to try to keep peace, but at the same time, I am not afraid of the person.

I am trained in the martial arts and I have taught the martial arts in the past, which really surprises people when they are told this, because I do not want any toughness to show.

When I became fearful for my relative's safety, at the right moment, I grabbed hold of the man's shirt, twisted it, and I wanted to push him against the wall, but there was a huge trash can between him and the wall, so I pushed him against the big trash can and threatened to beat him up if he would ever bother the young girl again. I said other things also. Imagine his reaction when a ninety eight pound woman who grabbed him, pushed him and talked tough to him! I almost pushed him over top of the trash can.

The restaurant would not open until 11:00AM, but I had to go to the ladies room myself.

I expected to see a woman in the ladies room, but instead, in the first stall, with the stall door open, was a big man standing there doing his business! All of a sudden a thought occurred to me. No one even knew I had walked into the building and yet, there was a big man standing in the stall with the stall door open and a big man standing outside the door.

A horrible thought came to me! What if that big man who I saw standing outside the door had followed me into the ladies room and I would be trapped between these two large men? I was suddenly prepared to fight! I quickly looked up into the mirror and much to my relief, no one was behind me.

I quickly ran out of the ladies room and the man was still standing there and he was watching the ladies room door and laughing and right at that moment, another big man came out of the men's room.

I quickly found the manager and told him and the manager found them walking out the door. You better believe the manager had a talk with them!

A very small girl went to work in a restaurant who knows the martial arts. No one who knows her would even suspect her as knowing the martial arts.

There was a man at her work place of whom all the young girls were afraid of.

This small girl was not afraid of him, even though she was much smaller in size than the man and the other girls.

The other young girls were afraid of this man, but not this young girl! Matter of fact, this man was afraid of this small girl! This small girl had even yelled at the man to leave the other girls alone.

One night an elderly man came in the restaurant with his wife and another woman.

He asked me if I had a relative that worked in a certain local restaurant. I replied that I did indeed have a relative who worked in the other restaurant. Then he got all excited because he was correct on what he thought, and his wife and the other woman kept asking him, "How did you know?"

This stranger saw my relative in the other restaurant then came into the restaurant where I worked and he made the connection between my relative and me. I'm not sure what the connection was, but he was correct.

One day the shift was getting close to changing. I saw a piece of paper under the table near a wall, so I got a broom to sweep it out.

As I was sweeping it towards me, I thought, "Oh, a customer dropped a dollar bill", but much to my surprise it was not a one dollar bill but it was a twenty dollar bill.

One time I found a fifty dollar bill, so I gave it to a manager. Since no one claimed it within one week, the money became mine.

Many times over the years, people ask me where I'm from because they hear me speak with an accent. Most of those people think I'm from England. I didn't realize just how English I sounded until one day four people from England thought I was from England.

I told them I was not from England, then the man said, I must be from the town of Smyrna and I told him I was and he said he knew I had to be either from England or that I was from Smyrna. I never thought that people in that small town ever spoke with an accent, but he said they did.

I got a delightful surprise on my fifty-fifth birthday.

In the restaurant, when it is someone's birthday we clap as we walk to the table, then we sing a birthday song as we put a birthday cake in front of the birthday person.

One my fifty fifth birthday I was told that singers were needed for someone's birthday, so I went to the back of the restaurant to join the other employees.

When I got back there, everyone started to clap and I was getting ready to clap when I suddenly realized that no one was moving. Suddenly, they started singing the birthday song to me! What a pleasant surprise!

One night an older couple was sitting in my section. Their total bill was $33.84 and the man put $120.00 cash in the binder which held the bill. He told me to keep the change.

When I picked up the binder to bring their change back I knew the man had made a mistake. I took the $120.00 back to him thinking he intended to give me forty dollars instead.

That started some "fireworks" because his wife didn't know her husband had a hundred dollar bill and she demanded to know where he got it from.

I quickly and very embarrassedly walked away.

When I first started waitress work I was surprised at how many young people I went to school with came to the restaurant to work, and they never seem to stay on the job very long, because they said the work was too hard.

I was shocked at first, but when I started thinking about it, I grew up on a farm, so I was accustomed to hard work. I always figured I did the hard work first and after doing farm work all other work is easy. It's possible they may have never worked a day in the lives!

Even today young people often tell me that I'm crazy for making restaurant work my career, but I really do enjoy this work. After all, I get plenty of exercise and I get paid for doing the exercise!

One day a man picked up his salt and pepper shaker and the lid was loose and a lot of salt fell on his plate. The pepper shaker lid was also loose.

Have you ever heard people who complain because their service in a restaurant was too slow?

Well, imagine someone complaining because the service was to fast! Yes, that actually happened!

We had a man come in every day who was from another country. This country where he was from is known for having a low opinion of women and this man reflected that opinion. He really enjoyed giving all the female wait staff a bad time.

This man got more cups of hot tea from one tea bag than anyone I have ever seen! He actually got five cups of tea for every one tea bag and he used about one whole lemon for every cup of hot tea.

One day he asked a waitress to rinse his tea bag. Now she was really angry, but he did it to see her get angry. He sat there and laughed at her.

What really makes my day? When customers walk through the door and ask to sit in my section.

I saw a young man with bright green hair. Was it Saint Patrick's Day? No, it was Good Friday.

Twins, twins and more twins! In one restaurant we had three sets of twins and two sets were identical twins. In another restaurant, we had two sets of identical twins.

Still, in another restaurant one set of identical twins came to work there. A young man working in the kitchen was not yet aware of the identical twins. One twin came into the kitchen and talked to him.

I wish you could have seen the look on his face and his reaction when both twins came into the kitchen together!

I worked in one restaurant that was owned by people from another country. They also hired people from their country.

One night a woman customer kept requesting more garlic bread, in which I had to keep going back to the kitchen and the cook had to make the garlic bread on each request. Finally, the cook said to me, "Oh you Americans! You eat so much bread and bread makes you stupid!"

I really don't think he was serious though, but he said it was because he was under a lot of stress because he was very busy and he had to keep making more garlic bread.

One time my employer had to call some of us back into his office. Somehow, his accountant had overpaid some of us and the overpayment would be taken out of our next paychecks.

Everyone complained about it except for me. Everyone felt they should not have to pay the money back because it was not their fault that they were overpaid. I felt that if I was overpaid then it was only right that I paid it back.

That next paycheck the over payment of $60.00 was not deducted from my paycheck. My employer told his accountant to let me keep the money. As far as I know, everyone else had to pay their overpayment back.

Imagine being pregnant, being at work then getting a phone call from the local hospital saying someone had been in a car accident with your children in the car and the emergency room wants permission to treat one of your children. Take my word for it, it's scary! The accident was nothing serious though.

One night there were three young people sitting in a booth, acting silly? All of a sudden the young girl bit the top of the head of the young man sitting next to her. Apparently, she bit him hard because he yelled, "Ouch! Why did you do that?" I didn't hear the reply because I was walking past the booth when I witnessed it, but I did hear her giggle.

Many years ago, we were required to get blood work and a chest x-ray so that we could get a health card to legally work in a restaurant. This was a state requirement.

A group of us went to a mobile unit when we got off work at 8:00AM. When we were standing in line, the group I was with talked as if they were afraid to get stuck with a needle, and I laughed at them.

When the person in front of me reached the woman to do the blood work, I saw blood fly across the room. I suddenly got scared and quiet. When it was my turn, I turned pale and everyone thought I was going to pass out when once again, blood flew across the room. I made it through the blood work and the chest x-ray and received my health card without passing out.

I was working with an older woman and she was just horrible to get along with! She really tried to make me angry and miserable. All of a sudden things changed and we became friends. I didn't know what happened until years later.

Years later, we were sitting with several other employees and we were talking. She started saying how she didn't like me when we first met. She said she was miserable on the inside and every time she looked at me I was smiling and it really bothered her. She went on to say that she actually picked on me to make me miserable, but every time she did those things I was still nice to her, so one day she decided, why keep trying to make me angry and miserable if it wouldn't work, so she decided to stop picking on me and she would be my friend. We had indeed become friends after that.

That was a real lesson for me. Ever since that night when I met someone who was mean and difficult to get along with I tried to turn them into a friend. I must confess though, there are a few people that were impossible to turn into friends.

One time a young girl and I were working on prep together, which means we were preparing food for the restaurant.

One woman we worked with would listen for the mixer to run then she would dash around the corner quickly when the mixer got quiet to see if we were making a cake. This would happen every time, but usually the young girl and I were working on prep alone, but that day we were working together. This woman always wanted to put several fingers in the mix, then grab the beaters, and stand there and lick the beater. This really disgusted the young girl and me.

This one day when the young girl and I were working on prep together, the manager had to make a dash to a local store for cake mix and several other items. This woman dashed around the corner and told the young girl and me that she wanted to know when we were going to mix a cake because she loved cake batter. When the woman left, the young girl asked me what we should do to keep this woman away. I thought for a minute or two then I came up with a perfect solution.

The young girl and I wore contact lenses, so I assumed that's why when we cut onions that the onions didn't bother our eyes, but other people couldn't even walk past the prep area without the onions bothering their eyes. Bingo! The answer to our problem!

When the young girl and I figured it was about time for the manager to get back with the cake mix and other items, we started cutting onions. It did the trick! The woman stayed away from the prep areas.

Some restaurants I use to work in had comment cards for servers to give to their customers. These cards the customers can fill out to let the management know about how they felt about their dining experience.

One time some young people wrote on a comment card "Free food for teenagers!"

Another time some customers came in shortly before closing time. One server was complaining that he hated customers that came in shortly before we closed but I told him that I didn't feel that way and that every customer was important. Apparently the customers heard our conversation, because they asked me for the male servers name and my name, then they filled out a comment card. They wrote on the comment card that the male server should be fired because he had a bad attitude and I should be given a raise because I had a good attitude about them coming in shortly before the restaurant closed.

Guess what! I didn't get a raise but the male server was fired!

We have a prison in the local area. One early morning a prisoner had escaped and the town police were notified that the escaped prisoner was probably on foot, so he could still be in the local area. While the town police and the state police were searching for the escaped prisoner, he was found in an unexpected place. The town police came into the restaurant for coffee and the town police saw the escaped prisoner in the restaurant sitting next to a large window eating breakfast! The escaped prisoner was getting a thrill watching all the police go by.

When I first started to do waitress work, the minimum wage for servers was 50¢ an hour and the minimum wage for other people was $1.00 an hour.

Now the minimum wage for servers is $2.23 an hour and the minimum wage for other people is $7.25 an hour.

The most number of hours I have worked in one day was sixteen and one half hours. Not bad, not bad at all!

I have had many young people tell me I'm crazy for enjoying restaurant work so much.

There are never two days exactly alike, I meet many interesting people. Many people pay "big bucks" to lose weight, but I lost a lot of weight because I do a lot of walking when I do waitress work and I don't have a lot of time to eat. Hey, how about that? I lost a lot of weight and I even get paid for it!

One day a woman employee called and said she couldn't make it into work. Reason? She said she had diarrhea so badly that she had to wash bed sheets several times and she had to take several showers. She had no diarrhea medicine in the house and she even had a trail of bowel movement from her bed to the bathroom. She wanted to know if we had any suggestions to help her. I told her of an old time remedy of things she should have already in her house. She tried it, and she seemed to think it helped even though she didn't make it work that day.

I get so disgusted hearing some servers with bad attitudes who complain about customers.

Hey, every customer is job security and I want a lot of job securities to walk through the door every day.

When a customer walks through the door of the restaurant, every employee they meet leaves an impression.

The most contact the customer has is with the server, so it is important that the server has a good attitude.

Now I realize some customers really are cranky and difficult to get along with, but the servers need to try to get along with them.

Every time an employee develops an attitude that they cannot be replaced, they end up getting fired.

An example is one young man I worked with who kept saying that he was the best server there and I kept telling him that pride comes before a fall.

The man even ran outside behind customers if he felt the tip was not enough and he would stop them from leaving in their vehicles, even threw the money back at them and tell the customers they had insulted him by not leaving more tip.

Guess what? He got fired!

In another restaurant another young man ran outside behind customers to tell them they did not leave enough tip.

My employer was there and saw the young man run out the door behind the customers and my employer asked other people what was going on and my employer was told what the young man was doing.

My employer waited for the employee to come back in. Then my employer asked the young man why he had run out the door behind the customer? The young man was so puffed up with pride that he told our employer the truth and the young man was fired on the spot.

One day an elderly lady asked me where the lavatory was. I had not heard that term in many years and I doubted if anyone I worked with would have known what she was talking about. What is a lavatory? It's a bathroom!

One time I went to my daughter's friend's birthday party in a restaurant. My daughter and her friends were having a good time. We sat down to eat our salad and wouldn't you know it, a piece of lettuce completely covered by wind pipe. I couldn't get the lettuce up or down and I couldn't breathe. I was so embarrassed and I didn't want anyone to know I was choking and I just sat there looking around. I thought I have gone through so much and now I'm going to die because of a piece of lettuce! Then I looked down and my eyes fell on my glass of water, so I picked up my glass of water and started to drink it. Much to my relief, the lettuce went down.

A wonderful thing happened to me one Sunday. A family came into the restaurant and they had seven children. The oldest was a teenager and the youngest was sitting in a high chair. I just had to comment to the parents, that they had such well behaved children. All seven children were very well behaved. I knew these parents were really doing a good job at raising their children,
They left the restaurant and not long after that, the mother of these children walked through the restaurant's door gave the roses to a hostess and requested the hostess give the roses to me then the lady left. It made my day!

When Nascar racing comes to town, the day of the races there are about 130,000 people that come to the area. In many parking lots and open fields, vehicles and RV's can park for a fee.
One race day a mother came into the restaurant. They lost their car and the mother asked me in which direction was the NASCAR race. She knew she did not park in the parking lot on the property where the

NASCAR races were being held, but her car was in another parking lot near the race track. I felt sorry for her and the children because she had many, many acres to look for her car. I bet she never lost her car again, ever!

A woman was so mean acting towards me at work. One day I decided that the only way to get her to leave me alone was to scream and yell at her. I know that even though some people there had known me for years, no one had ever seen me get angry. I am not saying that I cannot get angry, but that is an emotion that is difficult for me to feel. I screamed and yelled at her. Everyone was shocked, including her. After that day, we got along fine.

Several years later, she was going to quit her job and move to another state. Now it was my turn to get shocked.

She told me she knew she had been mean to me and she was sorry for her behavior. I thought I was hearing things because I could not imagine her telling me this.

This once again proves something. The best way to get rid of an enemy is to turn them into a friend.

A wedding reception was scheduled at the restaurant and we were told to expect fifty people, but only twenty two came.

I suspect the reason for the low turnout was because each guest had to pay their own way.

Only seeing eye dogs are allowed in restaurants, but pets are allowed on the patio.

One day a man brought his huge fluffy dog on the patio. This dog's fur was actually fluffy and when I say the dog was huge, I am not joking! This friendly dog had a lot of attention and when the dog's owner was asked how much the dog weighed, the answer was a whopping 163 pounds.

Now that's a big dog!

Talk about something different! A couple once told me that they had moved in this area about twenty eight years ago. When they moved here they went into one of these fast eating burger joints. They really like the salt and pepper shakers so as they were leaving they asked the manager if they could buy a set of the salt and pepper shakers. The manager said, "You want to buy a set of salt and pepper shakers? Wait here!" When the manager came back he gave the couple a set of salt and pepper shakers as a gift. The manager said he never had anyone ask to buy the shakers, but people would steal the shakers off the table instead. I would say this couple really made an impression!

A customer asked her server for a delicious dessert made with a large peanut butter cup.

When the customer took a bite of her peanut butter cup, she complained that the peanut butter did not taste like peanut butter.

Hey, have you ever heard of fake peanut butter?

A couple who sat in my section during a very cold day was a very interesting couple. They said it was a French toast day and I didn't know what they were talking about until they explained.

They used to live in the state of North Dakota and when they lived there they always knew when a snow storm was coming because the weather forecaster said it was a French toast day, so they knew to hurry to the grocery store. The items that disappeared first off the grocery store shelves were bread, milk and eggs.

What is French toast made out of? You got it! Bread, milk and eggs!

Hey, what is going on? A woman called the restaurant and said her daughter left her coat the day before and she asked if anyone had found the coat. No one knew anything about any coat being left in the restaurant.

She called again the next day and accused the employee's of the restaurant of stealing her daughter's coat and she said she had called the main office, since the restaurant was a chain restaurant and she also said she called the police. Hey, woman, how do we know that you even have a daughter or how do we know you were even in the restaurant?

Chapter Three

Dirt, Dirt and More Dirt

Thankfully, many restaurants are clean, but there are always those dirty restaurants as well.

No person's name or restaurants name is given to protect them in case we need a "barf bag" beside us.

I N ONE PLACE where I worked a young man came in and sat at the counter and gave an order for takeout. Now this was not unusual except for the young man himself.

He looked extremely dirty and his hair looked as if it had not been washed in many months. I did not walk any closer than necessary because I was afraid of the smell. I did notice however, that the entire time the young man sat at the counter, he was scratching his head and when he left the counter was literally black where he had been sitting.

People are filthy in public restrooms. The restrooms may be spotlessly clean, but a total disaster fifteen minutes later.

Would you believe that people throw paper towels and toilet tissue on public restroom floors! Why do people not want to flush toilets? Don't they flush their own toilet at home? Do they throw paper products on the floor at home? I should hope not!

Have you ever noticed how many people leave the restrooms without washing their hands, then we must touch the same door handle they do when we leave the restrooms? YUCK!

In one restaurant I worked in only on the weekends. When I went into work around 6:00AM to get things ready for breakfast the place was a total wreck from the night before.

The carpets and floors were also in a very dirty condition and there were even dirty napkins all over the floor from the night before and I knew the napkins were from the night before because of the food that was on those napkins.

I know one man quite well and his job requires him to sometimes go into the back of some restaurants. This man knows exactly which restaurants are clean and which restaurants are dirty.

One day he had a phone call where the person was saying that one of the restaurants telephone's was out of order, so he was to go there and repair the phone.

When he was checking out this restaurants phone in the back of the restaurant, he could find nothing wrong with it, so he decided to take the phone with him. Can you imagine what he thought as he was removing the phone from the wall, and cockroaches came pouring out of the wall? He said the cockroaches just kept tumbling out of the wall and then he realized that was why the phone wouldn't work.

I know of another couple who went out to eat. Every time eating utensils were brought to their table, the utensils had food stuck on them. Finally eating utensils were brought to the table that were, "passable."

The final thing happened when the wife was eating a bowl of soup when something in her mouth was not just right. When she investigated it, it was a piece of a wrapper from a package of crackers.

This couple said enough of this and they got up to walk out. One of the employees tried to stop them and the employee threatened to call the police and the man told the employee that was okay and he would even wait for the police, because if they didn't eat anything then why should they pay for anything? Then the man threatened to call the state board of health as they walked out the door. They have no intentions of ever going back there.

Now on the opposite side of things, image a restaurant where things are so clean that the health inspector will go in as a customer to eat.

I know of two places like that and it's a good feeling.

The ice cream machine for customers to serve themselves was not working, so someone was called to repair it.

When the repairman took the side of the machine off, cockroaches came running out of the machine and jumped on nearby customers who were eating and they panicked. I would have panicked if it was me who had a cockroach jump on me. The customers had their money returned to them.

Chapter Four

Robberies

Robberies can happen to any place of business, including restaurants. Most big robberies happen around Christmas time.

It would be nice if everyone could be honest, but they are not, so this chapter is about robberies.

Names and places are not mentioned here in order to protect the honest and dishonest.

P EOPLE WILL STEAL from anyone, even from servers.
One night I was walking behind several men who were walking toward the front door to leave the restaurant, when suddenly one man as he was walking past a table reached over and grabbed the tip off my table and he kept walking.

Personally, I feel it takes a really bad person to steal from someone who, at that time was earning only a little under $2.00 an hour, when minimum wage for other people was over $5.00 an hour.

One night four young men came in to eat. I was pregnant and working as cashier.

One young man got up and went to the men's room. The other three young men paid their bills then went out the front door.

When the young man came out of the men's room he dashed out of the front door without paying his check.

I ran outside and the other three young men were already peddling their bicycles across the highway.

Since I was pregnant I didn't "fight" too much with the young man as he was getting on his bicycle to peddle off to join his friends.

A few months later, I got a phone call at home to come into the police station and when I went into the police station I had to pick out the young man's photo out of a series of photographs.

When we went into court over the unpaid bill I discovered this young man was well known by the town police.

One policeman stopped the young man one day when the policeman saw the young man walking on the street. The policeman asked the young man why he didn't pay his food bill at the local restaurant. The young thief stuttered and stammer and he told the policeman and later to the judge in the court room on the day of the court trial. He gave the same reason to the judge that he gave to the policeman.

This young man said he just met the other three young men for the first time that night and the three young men invited this young man to the restaurant with them. This young man who was in trouble for not paying his bill said he thought the other three young men were going to pay his bill since he didn't have any money and they had invited him to the restaurant but apparently the judge didn't believe this young man any more than I did, because this young man had to pay his food bill plus court costs and he had to agree to never go into the restaurant again.

In the restaurant where I was working, there were men working there on a work release program from the local prison. Apparently, one man had not yet learned his lesson.

One night all the servers noticed when this certain man cleaned off their tables there was never any tip. I set a plot to catch the man.

I counted the money on my one table then I asked him to please clean off my table. When he cleaned my table, he told me there was no tip. I then confronted the man and asked him to give me my tip. He knew he was caught so he gave me the money that he had taken off my table.

I told the other servers immediately because they worked hard for their money and I didn't want any more of their tips stolen from them.

This man lost his job at the restaurant. I hope he has learned his lesson by now. It always pays to be honest.

At another restaurant years later, I was working with a woman who was desperate for money. She was so desperate she was seen taking money off another servers table. Such a pity when a person stoops so low!

One year when the restaurant was closed for Christmas, the manager got a surprise when she came back to work the day after Christmas.

The restaurants office was broken into and the money was stolen from the office safe. When an investigation was done, the robber was arrested and he served a prison term. He also just happened to be an employee.

My biggest surprise though was when my employer rehired the robber when he got out of prison.

One restaurant was robbed several times. I cannot even begin to imagine the horrors of being held up at gun point!

The town police said when one restaurant was held up, the police had never seen such hysteria among the victims. The reason for the hysteria was the beating the employees received from the robbers. It wasn't bad enough to steal; the robbers had to injure the employees! What a shame when people are so cruel to each other!

It was after midnight, and we were sitting in a booth talking when one waitress said, "You won't believe what I see!", as she was looking out the window.

There was a gas station with a small convenience store across the highway and a robbery was in progress. The robber was holding the employee at gunpoint while robbing the convenience store.

We quickly called the town police, but the robber was gone by the time the police got there. The employee was surprised to see the police there before he even called 911, so when he heard who called the police he called to thank us.

A drunken man came into the restaurant when the local bars had closed. After the drunk had eaten breakfast he decided to purchase a newspaper before he drove home.

The newspaper was in a metal box and a coin had to be inserted into a small box, then the front of the newspaper box could be opened. However, on this night, the newspaper box would not open after the drunken man had inserted his coins in the small coin box. Talk about racket! What a noise when the drunken man was banging the newspaper box up and down on the concrete floor in the foyer! Then out of pure frustration, the drunken man picked up the newspaper box and carried it outside and into his car, and then he drove home.

One of the kitchen workers was sitting in a booth eating and the kitchen worker wrote the drunken man's car tag number on a napkin. Not only did we have his car tag number, but this drunken man was a regular customer and several employees knew exactly where he lived.

We called the police and the police went to the drunken man's house and the police brought the newspaper box back to the restaurant.

One fast eating burger place I know about was robbed at the take-out window at the drive-through near Christmas time. Near Christmas time people will stoop to anything to get money!

One night one of the employees started walking out the back door when she saw someone trying to steal a battery from one of the employee's car that was parked at the back door. Caught in the act, the would-be robber fled.

In one restaurant I was working as cashier on the weekends during breakfast hours. Suddenly money started disappearing from the cash drawers, not only during breakfast hours but other hours also.

I was one of the people the general manager suspected of stealing money. There were people working there with whom I had worked with in another restaurant and all of them told the general manager that there was no way possible I would do something like that. The lady who was acting as manager during breakfast hours on the weekends had known me for only a few months, but she told the general manager that she really didn't believe any of us would be stealing money, but yet the only person she was willing to vouch for, was me.

Since money was being taken even when I was working on my other job, I knew it had to be someone who had access to the cash drawers at all times. Suddenly I realized who was stealing the money! It had to the general manager himself!

How I came to that conclusion was that I caught him stealing part of a servers tip and he knew I knew about it. I caught him in the act!

I quickly quit my job there. Not long afterward, it was discovered that the general manager was stealing the money and he was buying things for his house with the stolen money.

I'm sure glad I wasn't him when he was caught!

It amazes me how people try to get out of paying their bill. For example, one night I put the binder on the table with the bill in it for two young girls then I walked away. I no sooner walked away from their table then I turned around and saw them rushing through the front door. I knew something didn't look right, so I dashed over to their table and looked in the binder. Inside the binder was five dollars, but their bill was over twenty two dollars. Immediately I sprung into action. I ran, not walked to the front door, and out in the parking lot. They were fast and they were already very quickly pulling out of their parking space. They hit the gas pedal hard and raced to the back of the restaurant. I knew they thought there was a way to get out of the parking lot in the back, but surprise! They had no choice but to circle around the building to the front again, so I ran to the front of the building and waited. I thought I could at least get their car's tag number, but when they saw me, much to my surprise, they stopped.

The driver told me they didn't have enough money on them to pay their bill, so they were going to get the money and come back to pay their bill. They expected me to believe that!

I was starting to tell them that the other young girl could come back inside with me until the driver came back inside with the money, but the driver interrupted me and gave me her driver's license to keep until they came back. I told her I could not keep her driver's license in case she got stopped by the police, but I did write down her driver's license number and then I went inside the restaurant. I went straight to the manager and told him what had happened. As I was talking to the manager the town police walked into the restaurant to pick up an order of food that they called in. The manager and I went straight to the policeman and started talking to him and just about that time the one young girl came walking through the door and gave me the money and said, "We told you we would be back with the money." At least I got the money for the bill.

Chapter Five

Sad Things

If you kick off your shoes to sit in your most comfortable chair to read this chapter, you may need a box of tissues nearby for your eyes.

No person's name or restaurant's name is given in case you get to crying too hard.

I WAS WORKING one evening when suddenly an elderly man became ill. I have never seen a man turn such a blue color as he did. He was sick to his stomach and very, very blue. I was really scared that he was going to be dead before the ambulance got there.

The kitchen manager used to be a nurse and it just so happened that doctors were having a meeting in another room, so the ill man had help.

By the time the paramedics got there his normal color was back and I was so glad to see it. He was fine after that.

Many years ago I worked for a family that also had a car wash next door. One night my employer went to the car wash to collect the money. A man was there to rob my employer.

It just so happened that an older woman always walked out with a young girl to her car. This night the older woman was walking the young girl to her car when the two of them saw their employer being robbed. Now, this older woman had a lot of spunk and she ran into the restaurant grabbed her purse (which had a gun in it) and ran out the door, and ran next door to the car wash and she pulled a gun on that would-be robber and she yelled at the man who was trying to rob our employer. The young man fled without a single penny.

None of us were aware that the older woman had a gun in her purse until then.

Gun laws have changed a lot since then.

One Friday night when the restaurant was busy, I left the people's bill at one table. I immediately went over and started taking the order for another table. While I was taking the table's orders the people who had the bill that I just left with them got my attention as they got up to leave. They motioned to me that they were leaving the money on the table. I nodded to them and continued to take the peoples order. As soon as I was done taking the order I hurried over to another table that had two people sitting there and I took their order. Then I dashed over to the computer to put both orders in.

After I put both orders into the computer I turned around to dash over to the first table to pick up the money for their bill, but I saw the table had been cleaned off and there was no binder with cash in it. I could feel panic inside me as I almost ran to the hostess, but the binder wasn't there. Then I almost ran to find the bus boy to ask him about the binder, but I could see by his reaction that he had no knowledge of the binder.

Then the lady at the second table that I had taken the food order came up to me and told me that a certain man at the first table that I had taken the food order had taken the binder with the cash in it and he went into the men's room with it.

The manager went into the men's room and found the binder with the bill in it. The manager walked out of the men's room and walked up to the table and said someone had seen someone at the table take the binder with the cash in it off the other table and went into the men's room. He found the binder in the men's room with no cash in it. All the people sitting there denied that anyone even got up from the table.

The two people who witnessed the whole thing were angry with the thief and the man witness wanted so badly to punch the thief in the face, but his wife held him back!

Before the two people left that witnessed the theft, the man bent over the thief and told the thief that he saw what the man had done. The table of people made a noise that sounded as if to say, "Who us? Not us!", but we all knew the man was guilty.

It's really a shame when people are so dishonest. This happened just one week before Christmas.

Not only that, but they had small children with them, so they were a bad example to the children too. They were teaching the children to steal! How sad!

One shift in the wee hours of the morning there were several servers sitting in a booth talking because there was not a single customer in the restaurant.

Suddenly, these servers heard a commotion at the front door and when they looked in that direction, a young injured man was literally thrown through the front door. He was bleeding and bruised because he had been badly beaten, so while a server was taking care of the young man's wounds another server called the police and an ambulance.

The strange thing was that one young man who threw the injured young man through the front door had worked at the restaurant before and at that time several relatives of his were working there too.

The police went to the young man's house to arrest him and to find the other young men who were involved in the beating.

One day I stopped at the restaurant where I worked to get my paycheck. I opened the door to leave, but then I decided to turn around and say one last thing to a waitress. Good thing I did!

I got in my car and drove to the end of the parking lot and then I started to pull out. That's when it happened!

A speeding pickup truck did not stop at a stop sign. The pickup truck hit a small car that was traveling down the road alongside the other road that went past the restaurant. The restaurant was located on a corner.

A sickening crash was heard, the two vehicles slid directly in front of me and stopped in an open field.

The waitress and manager inside the restaurant thought I was in the accident and they came running outside, then the manager ran back inside to call for help.

The manager and I thought the young man in the small car was dead, but he wasn't, even though he was very seriously hurt.

The man driving the pickup truck who caused the accident was in a state of shock.

It just amazes me that if I had not stopped and said one last thing to the waitress before I went out the door, I could have very easily been in the accident myself.

Hopefully, the man driving the pickup truck learned a lesson; never run through a stop sign!

One night a fight started inside the restaurant between two men. One man had the other man's head wrapped around a coat rack at the end of the booth and the man whose head was around the coat rack was begging for help, while being beaten in the face.

A man who was sitting in another booth and who was a complete stranger to the two men got up and forced the one man to release his grip on the other man.

Once the grip was released on the one man the man who was being beaten ran out the front door so fast that I was expecting to hear the glass doors shatter.

The man who helped the beaten man never said a word, but he just went and sat back down in his booth.

The man who was doing the beating went back and yelled at the man who had helped the beaten man.

I was really scared that another fight would start, but the man who was yelling turned around and walked out the front door.

One night a young woman walked into the restaurant and asked if we knew where the man was that was riding the motorcycle that was parked in front of the restaurant. None of us knew where the man was.

She was calm, but she seemed to be almost in a daze and all of us were shocked by her appearance. A waitress asked her if she wanted us to call an ambulance for her, to which she replied she didn't and then she turned and walked out the front door.

The young woman was black and blue from head to toe and her face was terrible swollen.

I left about ten minutes later to go home and I saw her walking along the road.

The next evening we learned that she was badly beaten by her live-in boyfriend just minutes before she walked into the restaurant and the beating had taken place in the back parking lot of the restaurant.

We were shocked! If she looked that bad minutes after the beating, what could she possibly look like the next day?

Another time I opened the back door to the restaurant and I witnessed a young man hitting a young woman.

Shortly after I witnessed that scene, the young man and young woman came into the restaurant and she understandably was not speaking to him.

He asked me how far away they were from a certain town in Maryland. I told him they were about one and a half hours away. Now imagine riding with him in a vehicle for one and a half hours longer!

A neighbor woman of mine was telling me that when she was packing things in her car to leave her first husband, he came home. They got into an argument and she left in her car and he quickly jumped into his car followed her and then forced her car off the road, twisted her arm behind her back and forced her into his car. Then he drove about a half hour then they stopped at a restaurant, since she begged him to get her something to eat.

After they ordered their food the woman begged her husband to let her go to the ladies room which she had noticed his back was towards the restrooms.

A waitress was standing at the end of the counter and as my neighbor woman walked past the waitress, she quickly told the waitress to call the police because she had been kidnapped.

Needless to say, not very long after that the police walked into the restaurant and the problem was taken care of.

Three young men were sitting in a booth one day.

The waitress saw her tip on the next table, and then her tip was gone.

Since these three young men were acting silly the waitress took for granted that the three young men had taken her tip.

The waitress said out loud that the tip she saw on the table was missing, so she was going to have to check the video camera to see what had happened to it. There was no video camera but the three young men didn't know it.

The next time the waitress walked past the table the tip was back on the table and the three young men told the waitress they found her tip on the floor.

I might add here that no one else was sitting near the table where the missing tip was.

One young waitress was all the time telling her husband he should lock the car doors. One night she somehow neglected to lock her own car doors when she parked out back of the restaurant.

In the wee hours of the morning the town police called the restaurant for her. The town police knew all of us, because they came in the restaurant often.

The town police asked the waitress if she knew where her car was and she replied it was out back of the restaurant. The town police asked the waitress if she was sure of the car being out back of the restaurant, in which she told the police officer she was sure of it. The town police asked her to go check if her car was still there while they stayed on the phone.

She looked out back and sure enough her car was gone!

She came back to the phone and told the police her car was gone. The police told her they had her car. Several young men had stolen her car and since they were driving carelessly, the police tried to stop them, but it led to a high speed chase and the young driver wrecked her car.

The young men said they were going from car to car looking for an unlocked car door, then they found her car unlocked, so they "hot wired" her car then drove off in the stolen car. She was afraid to tell her husband since the doors were unlocked.

Have you ever known someone who has received their paycheck but there were not enough funds in the account to cover the paycheck?

Yes, I have known more than one restaurant where that has happened.

When that does happen not long afterwards, the restaurant always closes for financial reasons.

One night, two men started fighting inside the restaurant, so they were told that if they were going to fight they would have to leave the restaurant.

Both men left, but one man got to his car before the other man got to his car. The man who reached his car first, jumped into his car quickly, dashed out of the parking space in his car and deliberately ran over the other man while getting out of the parking lot. Of course, we had to call for an ambulance and the police for the hit and run accident.

One Easter, an older couple came into the restaurant and they wanted to know where the justice of the peace was located. I thought, "Oh, how sweet! They intend to get married today." Sad to say, that was not the case. They wanted to sue their son.

Some people make a living by finding reasons to sue, or to receive a free meal. Such was the case one day with a woman. She took food off the buffet then showed me a piece of glass, saying she found it in the food! The problem was that nothing was glass that was used to prepare the food.

I am very picky about keeping my vehicle doors locked.

One day my lock on my vehicle door was fine, however, when I left work to go home, it was a different matter.

I could not put my key in the lock and that's when I saw a sliver of wood hanging out of the vehicles door lock.

Someone had stuffed my vehicles door lock full of wood. I had to file a police report, and then get a locksmith to clean out my lock. I'm sure I know who did it, but I can't prove it.

One restaurant where I worked, truck drivers parked their rigs out back and came in to eat.

That was stopped when two women employees started dating the truck drivers and then one woman called a truck driver's wife and told her what was going on.

It was a big ugly mess! The trucking company also told the men if they were caught parking their trucks in the parking lot they could lose their jobs.

One Sunday morning and it just so happened that we changed our clocks so that I had nine hours of work instead of eight hours of work. No more daylight saving time!

It was around 7:00AM when all of us in the restaurant heard an explosion, then yet another explosion! The warehouse next to the restaurant was blowing up! Oh horrors! A man driving a gas truck was eating breakfast in the restaurant and his gas truck was parked next to the warehouse that was blowing up!

The truck driver risked his life to run out to his gas truck and move the gas truck! He was successful!

The town police and firemen came into the restaurant and told all of us, that we had to leave the restaurant so all of us had to stand out in the parking lot until it was safe to go back inside.

While working at banquets during wedding receptions, we can see a lot more than people think. It's really a shame to see some brides and grooms. Some marriages will not work.

For example, one couple was getting their picture taken by a hired photographer when it was over heard the groom saying to the bride, "Now please don't start anything (trouble) now!"

At another wedding reception, the maid of honor had gotten married the month before and her new husband who was also a member of the wedding party was flirting with other girls there at the wedding reception, and he even tried to make a date with one of the employees who was working that night. The maid of honor was in the ladies room crying and the bride and several other girls were trying to comfort the maid of honor.

People should never discuss how much tips they get. This causes jealousy. Servers will sometimes argue and really get rude to each other and to the host/hostess over who gets sat.

One night, I had a party of five people and my party had to use one table from another servers section. Since I used one of another servers table, if the need arises, then she could use one of my tales in my section.

Now, we work on rotation and when that party of five people left, it apparently was my turn to get sat again. I was told I was getting another party of five people in the same section.

The server whose table I was using told me this second party of five I was taking was supposed to be her party to which I replied that two hostess' told me it was my party. She said she knew that, but I had the first party of people, so now it was her turn, then she had the gall to tell me that if the hostess sat me another party of people that I should tell that hostess that it's not my party of people, but it belonged to her. This server already had a large party of people earlier that evening and even though I didn't count how many people there were in her party, I knew there were at least ten people in her one party of people. She also used two of my tables.

It amazes me how some people cannot do simple addition. When I went to school, 3+1=4, but when some people add the tip onto their credit or debit cards, 3+1=1.

There was an elderly lady who came to work as hostess. She tried very hard to be fair to everyone.

The servers who were accustomed to being shown favors, did not like this elderly lady and even accused this lady hostess as showing favors to me, in which she wasn't.

These servers really tried to make this elderly lady's life miserable.

When I was growing up, men never cussed, swore or used other bad language around a lady or child. It's sad to think, but today, young girls, women, (not ladies, just females), and children will cuss, swear and use other bad language. I hate the "F" word!

It's also sad to think, but there are very few gentlemen today. Many young men will allow a young girl to carry a heavy tray of plates while the young man will carry one or two plates of food.

I had surgery and I missed two weeks of work. When I went back to work I was not supposed to lift anything over ten pounds, for six weeks.

I had no pain or discomfort for two days by the time the six weeks were up, but I felt I needed another couple of weeks, before I should start lifting over ten pounds again.

I had a woman manager who was very difficult to get along with and she had very little compassion for anyone.

After not having any pain or discomfort for two days but yet the six weeks were up, this woman manager said in no uncertain terms that I was to lift over ten pounds.

I often wish I had stood up to her more, because lifting over ten pounds caused me to have pain and discomfort again and I did not feel better again for another year.

After working all these years in restaurant work, I have come to the conclusion there are three things that will destroy any workplace, not just restaurants, but any workplace.

One thing is gossip, not just any gossip, but "bad mouth" gossip. This is the person who just has to say bad things about everyone. Their "friends" should take something into consideration. The person who "bad mouth" gossips about everyone is also talking about them behind their backs.

Another thing that will destroy the workplace is a complainer. This person just has to complain about everyone and everything. One complainer can cause a lot of discord and unhappiness in the workplace.

The third thing that will destroy a workplace is a clique. Those in the clique are also guilty of "bad mouth" gossip and complaining. Anyone who is not in the clique is considered an "outsider." Those in the clique will cover for wrong doing of any member in the clique, but yet point an accusing finger at "outsiders". If they would just take a moment and think about something: whenever a person points and accusing finger at someone, there are three fingers pointing back at them. Go ahead, and try pointing your finger at someone. There really are three fingers point back at you! The "bad mouths" and "gossipers" also talk about their friends behind their back.

In high school, I had an elderly man teacher whom I really respected. He lived in a housing development which was behind where I worked.

After he retired from teaching, he came in where I was working nearly every day.

One day this elderly man walked through the front door with a blank look on his face and he said he could not get his car started.

One man sitting at the counter went outside to try to start the elderly man's car. Soon, he was back inside with a strange look on his face. He told us the elderly man's car was just fine, but the elderly man was confuse and could not find the ignition in his car. The good samaritan asked us if there was someone we could call to come and pick up the elderly man.

We knew the elderly man's wife was away visiting relatives in another state. The elderly man had an adult son who also lived in another state.

Since the elderly man lived in the housing development behind the restaurant, the good samaritan drove the elderly man home and made sure he got inside his house. Then the good samaritan walked back to the restaurant.

Imagine everyone's horror when the good samaritan no sooner sat down at the counter again, when the elderly man walked through the front door again saying that his car would not start.

This time the good samaritan drove the elderly man home while a waitress called the town police. The good samaritan stayed with the elderly man until the town police got the house.

We all had a fear that the elderly man would drive again and be involved in an accident and that's why the town police were called.

One night the restaurant was busy and we had a waiting list. In restaurant language, we were on a wait.

There was an older couple that came in.

A problem developed between the man and a hostess and the hostess tried to talk nicely to the man, but it did no good.

The couple got seated quickly and a manager talked to the man, but it did no good.

When the couple was leaving the restaurant, the man grabbed the arm of the hostess and called her a liar. It's difficult to imagine someone acting like that! A man actually grabbing the arm of a young girl and calling her a liar! She never lied to the couple!

There was a problem between a certain woman and me at work. Since I could not talk to this woman about the problem because she was so unreasonable, I went to the manager.

I asked the manager to please call this woman into the office so that the two of us could get the problem solved in front of the manager.

Much to my shock the manager looked at me and asked me why was I picking on her. I thought I was hearing wrong, so I asked, "What?" Again, he asked me why I was picking on this woman.

I was totally shocked! I just could not believe what I was hearing! Me, pick on her? There was a problem between her and me and I did not want the problem between us and that's why I went to the manager for help. I wanted the problem solved. Life is too short for things like this!

I knew the manager wasn't going to help, so I just walked out of the office. I knew the manager also knew better.

It's just a lot easier to work at getting along with people. Some people are just difficult to get along with, so it takes more effort to get along with them. Still other people are so cranky, no matter how hard someone tries to get along with them, it's impossible.

When people are fussing with each other, what happens? A persons stomach starts to hurt, they get headaches, can't eat or they overeat and they can't sleep. Is it worth it? No! It's just easier to put forth more of an effort to try to get along.

In one restaurant, an employer got very upset because an employee picked up her paycheck while she was working.

The employee was told that she was not being paid to pick up her paycheck.

A h h h h! How long does it take to pick up a paycheck?

Buffet style of restaurants seems to be popular, but yet they are going out of business. Why? People really abuse this type of restaurant by filling a plate with food, then they take one or two bites from the plate, then waste the rest.

People also sneak food in their pockets and purses. One time a woman was caught putting fried chicken in a large purse.

One night a young couple came into the restaurant on a date. Suddenly, she jumped up and ran out the front door crying.

What happened was that the young man just broke off their engagement and their wedding was just two days away.

It upsets me when a server is more interested in talking and listening to gossip than to greet a table of people when the people get seated in their section.

Every person that walks through the restaurant's doors is helping to keep the server's job. Every customer is extremely important.

It's so sad when employees do not want to accept new employees.

There was a new employee who came to work in the restaurant. One of the other employees who had been working there for a while would not accept the new employee.

I was standing a long way off when I heard a loud mouth employee yell in the back of the restaurant awful things about the new employee. The new employee ran in the back of the restaurant and started yelling at the loud mouth employee.

The loud mouth employee yelled a few things at the new employee then the loud mouth employee walked away while the new employee was yelling back at her.

That was bad enough, but what really upset me even more was that the loud mouth employee got away with behaving like that.

Employee's personnel files should be kept in a locked filing cabinet. The reason why I say this is because I have personally witnessed gossips going through the filing cabinets and they were going through the employee's personnel files. I have personally seen the same people doing this more than once.

I was hired as a cashier in one restaurant. It appeared to me on my first day that the woman who was supposed to train me was not anxious to do so.

On my first day, she showed me a little bit on what to do and after that whenever I asked her questions, she would dash over to my cash register and almost shove me aside physically and she would stand in front of the cash register where I was not able to see anything (she was very broad in size), then when she was done the transaction she would walk away. I would ask her to show me what she had done but she refused to acknowledge me.

One of the women servers knew me quite well from working with me at another restaurant. The general manager had told this woman server that he had asked my trainer how I was doing and my trainer had told the general manager that I wasn't doing so well. This woman server knew something had to be going on that no one knew about, so she casually asked me how I like my job and I told her exactly what was going on between my trainer and me. She immediately said, "I knew there had to be something going on!"

That's when I found out that I had replaced my trainer's best friend who was fired the day I was hired, so apparently my trainer was resenting me, because I took her friends place, so she didn't want to train me.

When the general manager came into work that day, the woman server told him what was going on with me standing there and he also had taken for granted that there was more going on than he knew about too.

This woman trainer and I were scheduled for different shifts after that and she quit her job about a month later.